MY FIRST LOOK AT VEHICLES

MOTORCYCLES COME IN MANY COLORS AND STYLES

Motorcycles

KATE RIGGS

CREATIVE EDUCATION

Published by Creative Education

P.O. Box 227, Mankato, Minnesota 56002

Creative Education is an imprint of The Creative Company

Designed by Rita Marshall

Photographs by Corbis (Sheldan Collins, Patrick Ward), Getty Images (Photonica, Roger

Viollet Collection), Hulton Archive, Derk R. Kuyper, Sally McCrae Kuyper, Craig Lovell,

Doug Mitchel, Wernher Krutein (photovault.com), Underwood Photo Archives, Unicorn

Stock Photos (Bachmann)

Printed in the United States of America

Library of Congress Cataloging-in-Publication Data

Riggs, Kate. Motorcycles / by Kate Riggs.

p. cm. — (My first look at vehicles)

Includes index.

ISBN-13: 978-1-58341-528-3

I. Motorcycles—Juvenile literature. I. Title.

TL440.15.R54 2007   629.227'5—dc22   2006018257

First edition 9 8 7 6 5 4 3 2 1

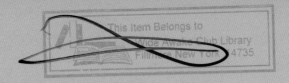
MOTORCYCLES

More Than a Bike

Motorcycles are bicycles with **engines**. They are much heavier than bicycles, though. They can go faster than bicycles, too. Motorcycles can zoom down streets just like cars!

Motorcycle rides are loud and windy. A motorcycle rider has to drive carefully. He also has to keep the motorcycle from tipping over! It takes good balance to drive a motorcycle.

MOTORCYCLES CAN GO ALMOST ANYWHERE

Motorcycles can go on roads or on dirt paths. People can ride them on long trips or short trips. Riders should always wear helmets wherever they go. Helmets protect riders if they fall.

THE FIRST MOTORCYCLES

A German man named Gottlieb Daimler (*GOT-leeb DIME-ler*) made the first motorcycle. He put a motor on a wooden bicycle. Daimler's son was the first person to ride it in 1885. Soon, other people wanted to make motorcycles, too.

In 1920, a motorcycle went
faster than 100 miles (161 km)
per hour for the first time.

THE FIRST MOTORCYCLE WAS VERY UNCOMFORTABLE

Two friends in America wanted to make motorcycles. Their names were William Harley and Arthur Davidson. The first motorcycles they made were too heavy. Sometimes they fell over and hurt the rider. These motorcycles were also very noisy.

Later on, people in Japan made motorcycles out of lighter metals. Many people liked these motorcycles. Riders could go really fast on them! And they were not as heavy.

Early Harley-Davidson
motorcycles weighed 900
pounds (410 kg) each!

"HARLEYS" BECAME POPULAR MOTORCYCLES

READY TO RIDE

People all over the world ride motorcycles. Many people in busy cities ride them. Small motorcycles let riders zip past cars on roads. Some countries do not have many roads. But cars need roads to drive on. It is easier to ride motorcycles in these places.

Some motorcycles can carry a **passenger** behind the driver. Other motorcycles have

Many police officers use motorcycles.

Motorcycles can get through

busy traffic easier than cars can.

room to carry stuff, too. People can put backpacks and sleeping bags behind the motorcycle's passenger.

Some special motorcycles have **sidecars** attached to them. Sidecars can be used to carry a passenger or things. People who like to travel a lot sometimes use sidecars.

Motorcycle sidecars were first
used during World War I (1914–1918).
They carried soldiers and weapons.

THESE MOTORCYCLES WITH SIDECARS ARE CARRYING SOLDIERS

RACE TO THE FINISH

Today, many people like to race motorcycles. Racers wear lots of protective clothing. They wear special suits and helmets. They wear gloves and kneepads, too.

There are two main kinds of motorcycle racing. Motocross racing takes place on dirt trails. Drag racing takes place on **paved** tracks.

RACING MOTORCYCLES ARE MADE TO GO EXTRA FAST

MOTORCYCLE RACERS LEAN TO THE SIDE TO GO AROUND CURVES

A drag race takes only a few seconds. That is because the motorcycles go more than 200 miles (322 km) per hour! In a motocross race, the course is much longer. Riders jump off ramps and zoom around sharp curves. Motorcycles are fun to ride or watch!

MOTOCROSS MOTORCYCLES FLY THROUGH THE AIR

Hands-on: Balancing Act

Riding a motorcycle takes balance. See how well you can keep your balance on wheels!

What You Need

A bike or roller skates

Beanbags (or plastic bags
    filled with rice)

Helmet

Sidewalk chalk

What You Do

1. Put your helmet on.
2. Draw a racecourse on a sidewalk or driveway with chalk. Make a lane about three feet (91 cm) wide.
3. Balance a beanbag (or plastic bag filled with rice) on top of your helmet.
4. On your mark, get set, go! Can you reach the finish line with the beanbag still on top of your head?

RIDING A PACKED MOTORCYCLE TAKES GOOD BALANCE

Index

Words to Know

engines—machines that make motorcycles move

passenger—a person who rides on a motorcycle but does not drive it

paved—a road that is covered with a hard, smooth surface

sidecars—little carts connected to the side of a motorcycle

Read More

Green, Michael. *Motorcycle Police*. Mankato, Minn.: Capstone Press, 1999.

Hill, Lee Sullivan. *Motorcycles*. Minneapolis: Lerner, 2004.

Siebert, Diane. *Motorcycle Song*. New York: HarperCollins, 2002.

Explore the Web

Bikes and Wheel Sport Safety http://www.nysgtsc.state.ny.us/Kids/kid-bike.htm

Motorcycle Mania http://www.kidscom.com/games/motorcycle/motorcycle.html

Vince and Larry's Safety City: Bike Tour http://www.nhtsa.dot.gov/kids/
biketour/index.html